Be A Problem-Solver

- - - - - - - - - -

A Resource Book For Teaching Creative Problem-Solving

Bob Stanish & Bob Eberle

Prufrock
Press

ISBN No. 1-882664-29-9

Introduction

The problem-centered thinking tasks contained in this book were prepared with a particular purpose in mind. By presenting whimsical problem situations, the authors hope that those engaged in the thinking tasks will be motivated to produce creative ideas that lead to the solution of problems.

The materials may be used in a variety of ways. Some of these ways are:

☞ Instructor-led activity with small groups as teams.

☞ Learning center activity with an individual working on his or her own.

☞ Take home activity with individuals working with selected others.

☞ Display material for generating student interest and motivation.

☞ Warm-up activity for problem-solving competition.

Suggestions for Using this Book

It is important that you take time to fully acquaint yourself with the methods and procedures involved in Creative Problem-Solving. To become familiar with the materials contained in *Be A Problem-Solver*, the following order is recommended.

Page 1 **Creative Problem-Solving Process.**
An overview of the steps of the process.
Notice the divergent and convergent phase at each step.

Page 2 **Whole World Creative Problem-Solving Assembly Line.**
A visual presentation of the CPS process.
Notice that each distinct step leads to the next step.

Page 3 **Whole World Creative Problem-Solving Assembly Line description.**
May be used in presenting page 2 visual to students.

Page 38 **How to Have a Mindshower.**
Rules to follow at the Idea Finding step.
Should be frequently presented to students.

Page 40 **User Guidelines for the Idea Evaluation Grid.**
A very important step in the process.
Guidelines must be followed as given.

Page 41 **Action Plans.**
How to follow through with a problem-solving idea.
Presents a host of techniques for gaining acceptance, and for implementing the selected solution to a problem.

Example: The example may be used as a point of reference when introducing the "Peeky-Poo Problem" to students.

Contents

Creative Problem-Solving Process

Being alert to situations in need of improvement.
Realizing that something should be done better.

A decision to work for improvement is made.
The challenge is accepted, a systematic response follows.

To get at the causes, questions are asked.
To improve understanding, data are collected.

Data are sorted, organized, and reviewed.
An orderly mess suggests problems and challenges.

Many problems and challenges are recognized.
The sub-problems are written as problem statements.

A bite-size problem is selected.
Problem stated in IWWMI (In what ways might I?) form.

Many problem-solving ideas are listed, judgment is deferred.
Far-out ideas are welcome, a quantity of ideas is sought.

Interesting ideas are given consideration.
Solution-promising ideas are selected.

Many criteria for judging ideas are listed.
Criteria are used to refine selected ideas.

Several important criteria are chosen to judge ideas.
Criteria are used to find the most promising ideas.

To activate ideas, determine what needs to be done.
Consider the needed steps. Prepare a step-by-step plan.

Most promising ideas are ready for use.
The step-by-step plan is prepared in final form.

Action plan is set in motion.

Reference: Isaksen, S.G. & Treffinger, D.J. *Creative Problem Solving: The Basic Course*, Buffalo, NY: Bearly Limited, 1984.

Be A Problem-Solver 1

The Whole World
Creative Problem-Solving
Assembly Line

Reference: Stanish, Bob & Eberle, Bob. *CPS for Kids*, Waco, TX: Prufrock Press, 1996.

The Whole World
Creative Problem-Solving
Assembly Line

1. The name of the machine in the illustration suggests that it has world-wide use. As a way of thinking and doing, it does have world-wide application. In fact, it is being used world-wide.

2. Starting in the upper left hand corner with "The Mess," and following through to the "Action Plan" in the lower right hand corner, the problem-solving machine illustrates the steps involved in being a creative problem-solver.

3. Notice the six steps in solving problems creatively. Each of the six steps may be learned and applied independently. They are, however, related to one another. Moving like an assembly line, one step performs a function that leads to the next step in line.

4. The assembly line is more than six steps performed in a set order. Taken as a plan, a scheme for dealing with perplexing situations, the six steps represent an organized, sophisticated, and efficient approach to solving problems creatively.

5. Creative Problem-Solving has the potential for making a positive difference in one's life. When learned and applied, individuals become more sensitive, resourceful, and self-sufficient.

6. Creative Problem-Solving makes it possible for individuals to use their full range of thinking ability. When this is done, individuals are better prepared to creatively meet the challenges that arise in their lives.

Creative Problem-Solving
Step-by-Step

Reference: "What To Do With Peeky-Poo?" pages 6-7.

I. **The Mess:** A situation that needs to be improved.
Peeky-Poo, your family dog, has a terrible habit. She takes dirty, smelly socks from the dirty clothes basket and places them in the laps of house guests.

II. **Data:** You get information as an aid to understanding.
You have scolded and punished Peeky-Poo, but she still maintains the habit. At times, you have placed her in a closed room, but she barks and makes it impossible for conversation to be carried on in the living room. When you place the dirty clothes basket on a table, she finds a way to knock it off and get the dirty socks. When dirty socks are sorted and placed inside the washing machine, Peeky-Poo has found a way to open the door and get them out. Your father is very upset with both you and Peeky-Poo and threatens to get rid of the dog if a reasonable solution is not found.

III. **Problem Statement:** Selecting and stating a manageable problem.
In what ways might I prevent the dirty sock problem from happening?

IV. **Idea Finding:** Listing ideas that suggest possible problem solutions.
- ❏ Get rid of dog.
- ❏ Get rid of father.
- ❏ Stop entertaining house guests.
- ❏ Give up wearing socks.
- ❏ Place muzzle on dog.
- ❏ Spray dog repellent odor on socks.
- ❏ Place dog in cage when guests come over.
- ❏ Put dirty socks in a safe until wash time.
- ❏ Take dog to obedience school.
- ❏ Spank Peeky-Poo with a dirty sock in your hand.
- ❏ Shampoo dog with dirty sock on your hand.
- ❏ Take dirty clothes to coin laundry every evening.
- ❏ Entertain guests on outside patio.

V. Solution Finding: Using evaluative criteria to judge promising situations. See page 41.

Idea Evaluation Grid

EVALUATION CRITERIA	CREATIVE IDEAS				
	Obedience School.	Coin Laundry.	Punish— bathe with a dirty sock.	Entertain on patio.	Put muzzle on dog.
1. Ease of doing.	3	2	5	4	4
2. Lasting effect.	5	1	4	1	1
3. Animal safety.	5	5	5	5	3
4. Family agreement.	5	3	5	2	2
5. Little cost.	2	1	5	5	4
TOTAL POINTS	*20	12	*24	17	14

* denotes most promising solutions

VI. Action Plan: Preparing a detailed plan for putting your ideas to work. See page 41, number 1.
1. Every week, family members take turns shampooing the dog using a dirty sock.
2. Take dirty sock from mouth of dog and spank her with it.
3. Pet and love the dog when she doesn't have a dirty sock in her mouth.
4. If successful, stop shampooing and spanking with dirty sock.
5. If not successful, enroll Peeky-Poo in obedience school.

What to do with Peeky-Poo?

Peeky-Poo, your family dog, has a terrible habit. She takes dirty, smelly socks from the dirty clothes basket and places them in the laps of house guests.

What to do with Peeky-Poo?

The Mess:
Peeky-Poo, your family dog, has a terrible habit. She takes dirty, smelly socks from the dirty clothes basket and places them in the laps of house guests.

Data:
You have scolded and punished Peeky-Poo, but she still maintains the habit. At times, you have placed her in a closed room, but she barks and makes it impossible to carry on a conversation in the living room.

When you place the dirty clothes basket on a table, she finds a way to knock it off and get the dirty socks.

When dirty socks are sorted and placed inside of the washing machine, Peeky-Poo has found a way to open the door and get them out.

Your father is very upset with both you and Peeky-Poo and threatens to get rid of the dog if a reasonable solution is not found.

Problem Statement:
In what ways might I prevent the dirty sock problem from happening?

Idea Finding:
Make a long list of ideas that suggest possible solutions to the problem.

Solution Finding:
Enter your five most promising ideas on an evaluation grid and measure them with the given criteria.

Criteria:
Ease of doing.
Lasting effect.
Animal safety.
Family agreement.
Little cost.

Action Plan:
See page 41. Select one or more of the given plans.

Terrible Tommy Toefoot

Barefooted and using his toes to turn pages, Terrible Tommy cheats on tests.

Terrible Tommy Toefoot

The Mess:
Barefooted and using his toes to turn pages, Terrible Tommy cheats on tests.

Data:
Tommy is the biggest, strongest, and meanest boy in class.

At test time, he places his textbook on the floor beneath the chair in front of him. With his shoe and sock removed, he can turn the pages with his remarkable toes.

You don't want to be a tattler, but you want Tommy to stop cheating.

Tommy plans to go to college and so do you.

Students in your class really like to stick together.

Problem Statement:
In what ways might you stop Tommy from cheating on tests?

Idea Finding:
Extend your thinking, go far out for ideas that have promise of solving the problem. Come up with a long list of ideas.

Solution Finding:
Listed below are criteria to be used in the evaluation of your selected ideas. Use an evaluation grid to judge your ideas.

Criteria:
Avoids tattling.
Avoids a fight.
Ease of doing.
Immediate results.
Agreeable to Tommy.

Action Plan:
It may take some doing to put your idea into action. You will need to think it through each step of the way. See page 41.

Down the Drain

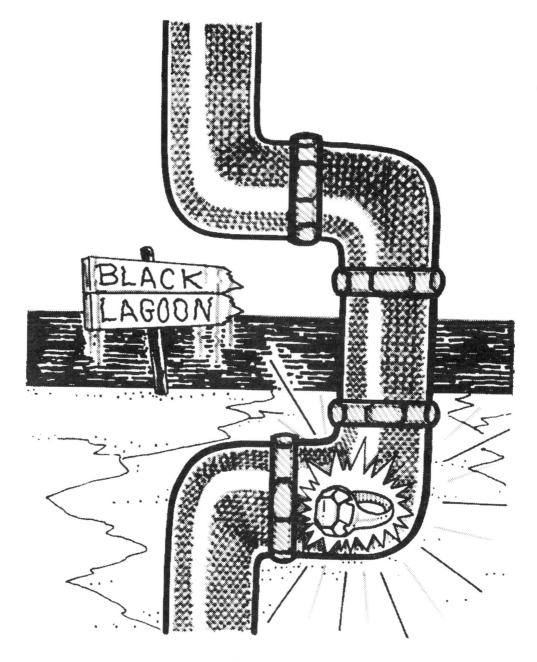

A priceless diamond ring has been lost down the drain.

Down the Drain

The Mess:
A priceless diamond ring has been lost down the drain.

Data:
The drain pipe leads to a dark lagoon.

Nothing has ever been recovered from the lagoon.

The pipe has a diameter of four inches.

The pipe is made of cast iron.

In one hour, water will flush through the pipe.

The priceless diamond has a solid gold setting.

The ring is in the next to the last elbow before it drains into the dark lagoon.

Problem Statement:
In what ways might I recover the ring?

Idea Finding:
Accept all ideas that come to mind. Then, make a long list of ways to recover the ring.

Solution Finding:
Check over your ideas and select the five that offer the greater promise for recovering the ring. List them on the evaluation grid and measure them using the given criteria.

Criteria:
Time.
Cost.
Damage to pipe.
Safety of diamond ring.
Ease of doing.

Action Plan:
Page 41 suggests a number of action plans. Make a choice of one or more, then go ahead with your plan.

My Friend Cyclops

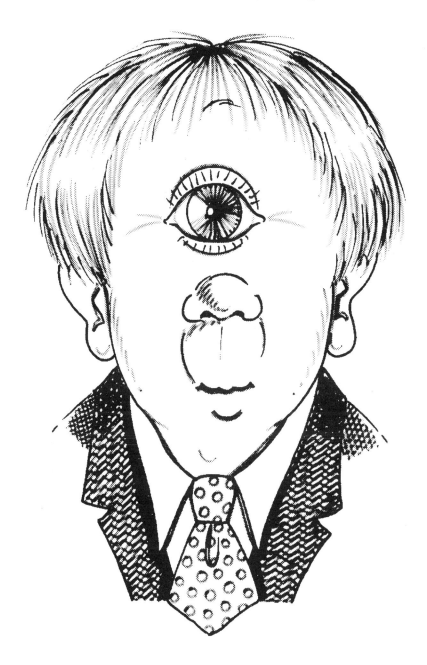

Cyclops has lost his contact lens.

My Friend Cyclops

The Mess:
Cyclops has lost his contact lens.

Data:
With only one eye, the lost lens is a problem.

Cyclops is a friend of yours.

When you phone your friend, you learn of the lost contact lens.

Cyclops asks you to help him find the lens.

Cyclops lives 20 minutes from anyone.

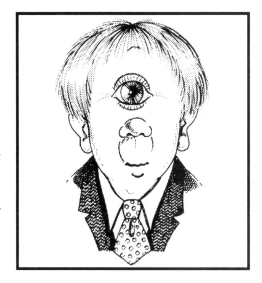

Without his lens he cannot see well enough to drive a car or dial the phone.

He is low on money and the electricity in his house has been cut off.

He has an important job interview in 45 minutes.

Cyclops has astigmatism.

Problem Statement:
In what ways might I, or we, go about finding the lost lens so that Cyclops will make it to his interview on time?

Idea Finding:
Taking the data into consideration, list all of the possible ways you can think of for finding the lost contact lens.

Solution Finding:
Take your five most promising ideas and enter them on an evaluation grid. Use the given criteria to rate them.

Criteria:
Time.
Lens safety.
Practicality.
Cost.
Cyclops' feelings.

Action Plan:
Show and/or tell how you will make your plan work by using one or more of the suggestions given on page 41.

How to Stop a Nuthead?

When you are home alone, you frequently get prank telephone calls from the same nuthead.

How to Stop a Nuthead?

The Mess:
When you are home alone, you frequently get prank telephone calls from the same nuthead.

Data:
The prank phone calls bother you.

Whoever calls seems to know that you arrive home from school at 3:30 p.m.

Your brother plays soccer, and he arrives home around 4:15 p.m.

Both of your parents work and arrive home after 5:15 p.m.

Your mother works at the bank. Your dad sells insurance. It is important that you relay incoming business calls.

The phone company was notified, and they offered to install special equipment.

Due to the nature of his business, your dad will not allow the special equipment.

Problem Statement:
In what ways might you stop the calls from the nuthead and still be able to relay important business calls to your parents?

Idea Finding:
Can you list 15 ideas? 20 ideas? How about 25 ideas? Think to produce many ways to solve this problem.

Solution Finding:
Taking the evaluation criteria given, enter your ideas on an evaluation grid and judge them.

Criteria:
Ease of doing.
Cost.
Agreeable to you.
Continued phone service.
Agreeable to family.

Action Plan:
Think through the plan you will use to activate your idea. Get the help you may need by checking out page 41.

Be A Problem-Solver   15

Squeaky Shirley

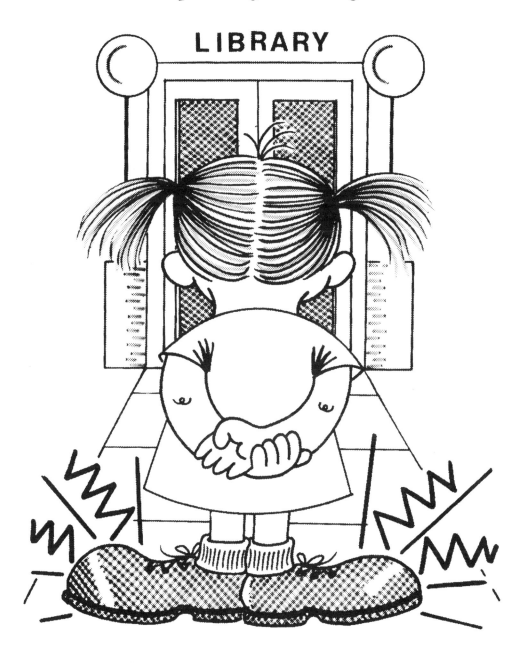

Shirley Squeak has squeaky shoes and is not allowed to enter the library to prepare her research paper.

Squeaky Shirley

The Mess:

Shirley Squeak has squeaky shoes and is not allowed to enter the library to prepare her research paper.

Data:

The research paper is due in a week, and it must be typed.

The library does not allow squeaky shoes, barefeet, or stocking feet.

The Squeak family is notorious for putting things off until the last minute.

Shirley has one hour to gather information before the library closes.

Information can be found in reference books that cannot be checked out.

The library has a copy machine. Shirley has $1\frac{00}{}$ worth of change.

Shirley's parents have gone shopping and will return home after 9:00 p.m.

Shirley's aunt will pick her up when the library closes at 9:00 p.m.

The library has a pay phone.

On Saturday night, it takes her aunt 30 minutes to drive to the library.

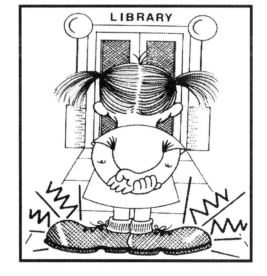

Problem Statement:

In what ways might Shirley get information without breaking library rules?

Idea Finding:

Go far out and come up with as many problem solutions as possible.

Solution Finding:

Enter your five most promising ideas on an evaluation grid and rate them.

Criteria:

Time.
Library rules.
Cost ($1\frac{00}{}$ maximum).
Ease of doing.
Quality of effort (job well done).

Action Plan:

See page 41 for ideas. Then, go ahead with your plan.

The Weird World of Wumbas

A rare wumba is slowly sinking in quicksand.

The Weird World of Wumbas

The Mess:
A rare wumba is slowly sinking in quicksand.

Data:
Wumbas are rare, almost extinct beasts.

A full grown wumba weighs about two tons.

Standing, a wumba is about 25 feet tall.

Wumbas live on citrus fruits and juices.

Water frightens wumbas.

About $\frac{1}{3}$ of the wumba is still exposed.

It is estimated that the wumba is sinking six inches every hour.

Studies show that wumbas are subject to sudden heart attacks.

When around human beings, the pulse rate of a wumba increases.

A generous reward is offered to anyone who saves the wumba.

Problem Statement:
In what ways might the wumba be saved from almost certain death?

Idea Finding:
You will need to be clever and resourceful to solve this problem. The right time for evaluating your ideas will come later. Right now, make a long list of wumba-saving ideas as they come to mind.

Solution Finding:
Select your five most promising ideas and enter them on an evaluation grid.
Using the given criteria, assign points to determine which ideas are best.

Criteria:
Cost.
Time.
Safety to the wumba.
Ease of doing.
Suits the situation.

Action Plan:
See page 41 for action plan ideas.
Determine the plan you will use and follow through with your selected plan.

Stalled at the Mall

With your wallet locked in the car, you are stalled from seeing the movie at Westgate Mall.

Stalled at the Mall

The Mess:
With your wallet locked in the car, you are stalled from seeing the movie at Westgate Mall.

Data:
Your mom has driven you to Westgate Mall to see a movie with a friend.

Your aunt picked up your mom, and they went out of town to visit relatives.

You have no money to see the movie. Your wallet is locked in the car.

Your mom will return in three hours. Your dad is out of town on business.

You have $4^{00} in your wallet. The movie costs $2^{50}.

You had planned to spend the money leftover on popcorn and a drink.

A locksmith in the mall would charge more than you have to open the car door.

The car window on the passenger side is open by one full inch.

The movie starts in 20 minutes.

Problem Statement:
In what ways might I recover the wallet from the car before the movie starts?

Idea Finding:
Explore the many possible ways of recovering the wallet from the locked car. Treat all ideas kindly and list them as they come to mind.

Solution Finding:
Enter your best ideas on an evaluation grid. Judge them with the criteria given.

Criteria:
Cost.
Time.
Ease of doing.
Not damaging the car.
Effect on me.

Action Plan:
Draw up your plan using suggestions given on page 41.

The Undoing of Four-Fang

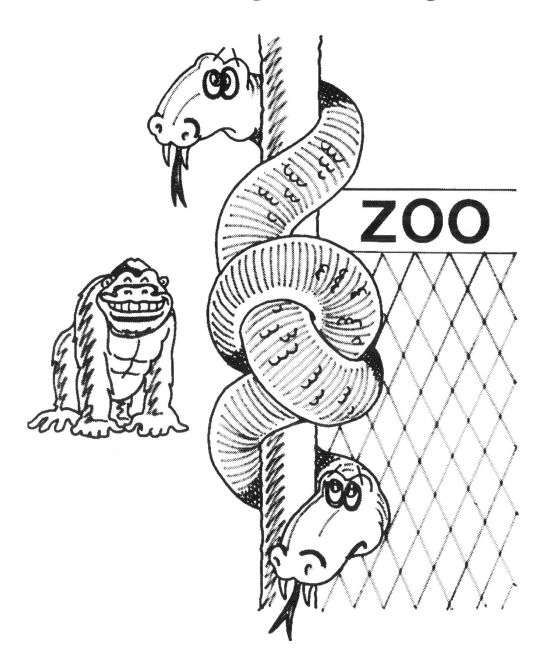

Four-Fang, a prized, two-headed snake, has been tied into a knot by Gadzilla, the most feared gorilla in captivity.

The Undoing of Four-Fang

The Mess:
Four-Fang, a prized, two-headed snake, has been tied into a knot by Gadzilla, the most feared gorilla in captivity.

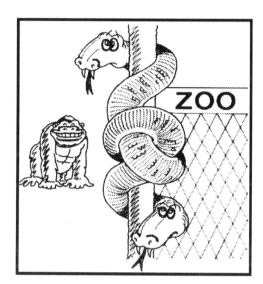

Data:
Four-Fang is 20 feet long.

The bite of either head is deadly.

Gadzilla is immune to snake bites.

Four-Fang is a one-of-a-kind snake.

Millions of people come to the zoo each year to see Four-Fang.

When tied in a knot, Four-Fang cannot sleep or digest food.

Without the snake on display, a great deal of money from admission fees would be lost. If the snake is not untied, it only has a month to live.

Problem Statement:
In what ways might I bring about the undoing of Four-Fang?

Idea Finding:
Let your thinking strike out in many directions as you list problem-solving ideas. Welcome all ideas as you create a long list.

Solution Finding:
Using an evaluation grid, enter the given criteria as you go about the task of selecting your best idea.

Criteria:
Cost.
Time.
Avoids crowd disturbance.
Risk to human beings.
Safety of Four-Fang.

Action Plan:
After selecting a solution to the problem, you are ready to come up with a plan for carrying it out. See page 41 for action plan suggestions. Determine the plan you will use and go ahead with it.

Forgotten Trip Slip

You forgot to get a parent permission slip to go on the class field trip. As your teacher collects the slips, you make this disgusting discovery.

Forgotten Trip Slip

The Mess:
You forgot to get a parent permission slip to go on the class field trip. As your teacher collects the slips, you make this disgusting discovery.

Data:
Your school has a strict policy requiring signed parent permission slips.

Many of your school friends are going on the trip, and you also wish to go along.

You don't want to spend the day in the school's media resource center.

Your parents are at work. Your father is a pilot for a crop dusting company. Your mother is a computer programmer for a software firm.

The driving time from each of your parent's work is 45 minutes.

The school bus will travel in the opposite direction from your parents' work.

It is now 8:15 a.m.; the bus will leave at 9:00 a.m.

You really want to go on the trip. It appears that you will be left at school.

Problem Statement:
In what ways might you meet the parent permission requirement to go on the trip?

Idea Finding:
Use your wits and resources in listing ideas to lead to a problem solution.

Solution Finding:
Enter ideas and criteria on an evaluation grid. Award points to determine your best working idea.

Criteria:
Ease of doing.
Cost.
School policy.
Effect on parents.
Effect on you.

Action Plan:
For ideas, see page 41. Prepare your plan and follow through with it.

Not in the Lease

Bruce, all 150 pounds of him, has moved into an apartment with you. Your lease has a restriction of 15 pounds of pets per apartment.

Not in the Lease

The Mess:
Bruce, all 150 pounds of him, has moved into an apartment with you. Your lease has a restriction of 15 pounds of pets per apartment.

Data:
Bruce is in your care while his owner is in the hospital.

You are aware of the 15 pound pet restriction spelled out in the lease.

You don't have the money to pay someone to keep Bruce.

All of your friends live in apartments with similar lease restrictions.

Bruce is a kind soul, but he makes loud responses to train whistles. Every night at 12:05 a.m. a freight train passes.

Bruce's owner will return home in two weeks.

There are four months left in your lease.

Problem Statement:
In what ways might you keep Bruce in your apartment for two weeks without losing your lease?

Idea Finding:
Explore all possibilities. Let your thinking go in many directions as you list ideas that may lead to a problem solution.

Solution Finding:
Take your most promising ideas and list them on the evaluation grid. Then, take the given criteria and judge them.

Criteria:
Cost.
Effect on Bruce.
Effect on apartment tenants.
Suits the situation.
Will last for two weeks.

Action Plan:
What needs to be done to make your plan work? Consider the details involved. For help in designing your action plan see page 41.

The Saga of the Sandspoon

The sandspoon makes your parents furious when it deposits piles of sand on the floorboard of the family car.

The Saga of the Sandspoon

The Mess:
The sandspoon makes your parents furious when it deposits piles of sand on the floorboard of the family car.

Data:
When your family goes to the beach, the sandspoon loves to go along with you.

Sandspoons have feet shaped like tablespoons that fill up with sand.

When petted, sandspoons relax.

In the car, the sandspoon likes to sit on your lap.

Sandspoons' feelings are easily and frequently hurt.

The weight of a sandspoon is about 75 pounds.

Returning from the beach, the sandspoon relaxes and deposits sand in the car.

When your parents become furious with the sandspoon, they take it out on you.

Problem Statement:
In what ways might you avoid getting sand in the floorboard of the car without hurting the feelings of the sandspoon?

Idea Finding:
Play around with fantastic ideas. List all the ideas you can think of.

Solution Finding:
To find a solution, enter ideas and criteria on an evaluation grid. Award points to determine the best idea.

Criteria:
Parent satisfaction.
Lasting effect.
Ease of doing.
Sandspoon's feelings.
Safety of the sandspoon.

Action Plan:
See page 41. Plan your work, then work your plan.

Fabulous Freddie

The aroma of spaghetti meat sauce causes Freddie to become ill.

Fabulous Freddie

The Mess:
Fabulous Freddie, your friendly frog, is truly a great pet. However, when he sits on the edge of your dinner plate, the aroma of spaghetti meat sauce causes him to become ill.

Data:
Freddie is a well-behaved frog.

He has been your pet for three years.

He loves to be near you and to sit on the edge of your plate when you eat dinner.

Your parents don't mind Freddie being at the table as long as he behaves.

Spaghetti with meat sauce is one of your favorite meals.

The aroma of the meat sauce makes Freddie extremely ill.

Your plate is loaded with spaghetti without meat sauce.

You are very hungry and you want to start eating your favorite meal.

The dish of meat sauce is sitting in the middle of the table.

Problem Statement:
In what ways might you go about enjoying your spaghetti with meat sauce without harming or disturbing Freddie sitting on the edge of your plate?

Idea Finding:
Consider the data, then list unusual but workable solutions to the problem.

Solution Finding:
Enter ideas on an evaluation grid and measure them with the criteria given.

Criteria:
Ease of doing.
Parent agreement.
Cost.
Frog agreement.
Effect on you.

Action Plan:
Taking the ideas you selected, prepare a plan to put into action. Choose from the list of plans on page 41.

The Case of the Messy Dwibble

"The Dwibble" makes a mess of the bathroom and your mother is tired of the extra work she has to do.

The Case of the Messy Dwibble

The Mess:
"The Dwibble" makes a mess of the bathroom and your mother is tired of the extra work she has to do.

Data:
Your parents have given their permission for a friend to stay with you for three weeks.

Your friend's parents are on vacation.

Your friend likes to shower several times a day. Afterward, the bathroom is a mess.

Your mother finds water on the floor and a pile of dirty towels after each shower.

At the end of the first week, your friend is being called "The Dwibble."

"The Dwibble" takes a shower every afternoon at 1:30 p.m. and at 2:30 p.m.

You have part-time job that starts at noon and ends at 5 p.m.

Your mother's garden club meets at your house on Wednesdays from 3-5 p.m.

On the 10th day of the visit, your mother said, "The Dwibble has to go. I can't take this mess any longer!"

Problem Statement:
In what ways might you arrange for your friend to remain for the rest of the visit and not have a continual mess in the bathroom?

Idea Finding:
With no restrictions on wild ideas, list all the possible solutions you think of.

Solution Finding:
Judge your selected ideas using an evaluation grid and given criteria.

Criteria:
Cost.
Time.
Lasting effect.
Will not hurt friend's feelings.
Agreeable to mother.

Action Plan:
Check out page 41, then go ahead and detail your plan.

Heartthrob!

You would like to meet Heartthrob, but you don't know how to go about it.

Heartthrob!

The Mess:
You would like to meet Heartthrob, but you don't know how to go about it.

Data:
In class, you can't keep from staring at Heartthrob.

You're too shy to start a conversation.

There is a school dance in three weeks.

Heartthrob is new in school and doesn't have many friends.

You really would like to spend some time with you-know-who.

You're not sure if Heartthrob has noticed you.

Problem Statement:
Finding yourself in somewhat of a mess, you have a challenge on your hands. What are some of the things you want to happen? Let them be sub-problems, and write them as problem statements.

List at least three IWWMI statements.
In what ways might I _____?

Select one of your IWWMI statements for creative attack with the steps of the Creative Problem-Solving process.

Idea Finding:
Let your imagination soar as you list creative ideas. Go far out and respond to your IWWMI statements.

Solution Finding:
First, make a list of criteria you will use to evaluate your ideas. Next, take the criteria and enter them on an evaluation grid. Then, enter your ideas on the grid and evaluate them.

Action Plan:
Check out page 41 for ideas. Determine the plan you will use and carry it out.

Nobody Notices Nerdferd

Nerdferd goes to extremes to gain attention.

Nobody Notices Nerdferd

The Mess:

Nerdferd goes to extremes to gain attention.

Data:

Most of the time, Nerdferd is ignored by others.

In appearance and manners, he is not an attractive person.

Once you get to know him, he is really a great guy.

To gain attention, he eats wooden rulers and makes disruptive croaking noises.

On several occasions, he has come very close to getting thrown out of school.

As a friend, you are concerned that he will be thrown out for good.

You have tried to convince Nerdferd to cool it, but he continues to go to extremes.

Problem Statement:

As you study the data, it is clear that a complicated situation exists. As it involves Nerdferd, there are matters of self-respect, disruptive behavior, and acceptance by others.

Select the sub-problem you will work with and phrase it in an IWWMI statement.

In what ways might I _____?

Continue on your own with the remaining steps of the problem-solving process.

Idea Finding:

Solution Finding:

Action Plan:

How to Have a Mindshower

When you want to think of ways a problem might be solved, you ask your mind to "shower down" a lot of ideas. To have a productive shower and have your mind pour out ideas, there are some rules you need to follow.

👉 **Be a friend to ideas.** Don't make fun of anyone's ideas, including your own. Welcome all ideas and put them on your list, even if they don't seem to be very good at the moment. Later, you will have the chance to judge your ideas.

👉 **Build a bunch of ideas.** Go for a long list of ideas. The more ideas, the better. When you think the rain of ideas is about to stop, crank up your mindshower machine and pour out 10 more ideas.

👉 **Favor far-out ideas.** Crazy, wild, far-out ideas may lead you to a problem solution. By working over a far-out idea you may tame it down so that it is both respectable and workable.

👉 **Ping-pong ideas.** Take your ideas, and the ideas of others, and bounce them back and forth in your mind like a ping-pong ball. Soon, one idea will lead to another, then another, and another. By pinging and ponging one idea, you may end up with 10 more.

Idea Evaluation Grid

EVALUATION CRITERIA	CREATIVE IDEAS				
1.					
2.					
3.					
4.					
5.					
TOTAL POINTS					

Rating Scale:
5 points — Excellent idea.
4 points — Good idea.
3 points — Average idea.
2 points — Below average idea.
1 point — Poor idea.

User Guidelines
for the Idea Evaluation Grid

1. Ideas selected for evaluation are listed in the spaces provided across the top of the grid.

2. Criteria to be used in evaluating selected ideas are listed in the spaces provided down the side of the grid.

3. Starting with the first criteria listed, judge each idea across the page using only the first criteria.

4. Proceed with the evaluation by moving to the second criteria. Again, make comparisons and award points across the page. Continue in this manner using all listed criteria.

5. After all criteria have been applied to all ideas and points awarded, add the points awarded to each idea and enter the total in the spaces provided at the bottom of the grid.

6. Ideas receiving the greater number of points should be considered for acceptance value and implementation.

	CREATIVE IDEAS				
EVALUATION CRITERIA					
1.					
2.					
3.					
4.					
5.					
TOTAL POINTS					

Note: When using the rating scale, a spread of points does not have to be awarded across the grid. This is to say that more than one idea may receive a 5. Likewise, it may be that none of the ideas receive 5 points.

Rating Scale:

5 points	Excellent idea.
4 points	Good idea.
3 points	Average idea.
2 points	Below average idea.
1 point	Poor idea.

Action Plans
Who? What? Where? When? Why? How?

Your plan for carrying out the problem solution should answer the above questions.

1. Prepare a detailed, written plan for implementing your problem solution.
2. Using a tape recorder, dictate your plan step-by-step.
3. Draw a cartoon sequence that visually explains your idea.
4. Do a puppet show that tells the mess and acts out the solution.
5. Compose song lyrics to describe your plan. Sing your plan to a familiar tune.
6. Present your plan in pantomime.
7. Draw a flow chart of your plan on large paper or poster board.
8. Write and perform a play that explains the mess and how the problem was solved.
9. Should an invention be involved, construct it and demonstrate its' use.
10. Prepare a time line of events for carrying out your action plan.
11. Write and illustrate a children's book. Have it show the steps of CPS.
12. Perform an interpretive dance to music that would help to explain your plan.
13. Present your plans using felt tip pens and a flip chart with newsprint.
14. Prepare and show a film strip that pictures your action plan.
15. Make some transparencies and use with a projector for a visual presentation.
16. Should an object be involved, be the object and demonstrate the steps of CPS.
17. Using old magazines, construct a collage of words and pictures to outline a plan.
18. In chart form, list crucial questions and provide the answers.
19. Write a newspaper story. Describe the mess and your creative solution.
20. Use any of the above ideas in combination to come up with a different plan.

Be creative and design a plan that is different from those given above.

References

Elwell, Patricia A. & Treffinger, Donald J. *CPS for Teens: Classroom Activities for Teaching CPS*, Waco, TX: Prufrock Press, 1993.

Isaksen, S.G. & Treffinger, D.J. *Creative Problem Solving: The Basic Course*, Buffalo, NY: Bearly Limited, 1984.

McIntosh, Joel E. & Meacham, April W. *Creative Problem Solving in the Classroom: A Teacher's Guide to Effectively Using CPS in Any Classroom*, Waco, TX: Prufrock Press, 1992.

Stanish, Bob & Eberle, Bob. *CPS for Kids*, Waco, TX: Prufrock Press, 1996.